7 Big Steps to a Better Life

Magic Wand in Your Hands.

Use It!

CLAUDIA NITA DONCA

God is in all men, but all men are not in God. This is why their suffering.
(Ramakrishna)

CONTENTS

INTRODUCTION

I have always wondered how I could transmit my knowledge concerning spiritual practices to my loved ones, or to anyone who needs it. Each soul living on this Planet is daily searching for spiritual knowledge, for its own soul's evolution. Some of us find it in our pertaining religion; others find it in a spiritual teaching which attracts us and others in an impact happening from our life, or simply in a prayer. None of the above mentioned ways are wrong, as long as we reach the final goal: spiritual growth, because this is our main objective in our earthly lives.

Ten years ago, I have began the journey with an open soul, towards a spiritual practice which I thought would be what I needed to "open my eyes" and see the world, to understand the purpose of my life, to learn how to raise my child as well as I could... Exercising and practicing, I understood basic spiritual notions and I gained a greater thirst for knowledge. Each year which passed by brought up a better understanding of other systems which completed my knowledge, till I reached the "magical" number 7, considered by numerologists as a divine number.

Then the Magic happened: "the declick" which helped me get to know myself better and understand the great Truth, that real knowledge lies within ourselves, within our soul, in the cleanest little room, which is the Divine Spark received by us at birth. The spiritual practices have the role to wake us up and use the great force already present in each of us! And believe me, each of us has it, but we aren't all aware of it...

This huge inner FORCE is based on the Divine Truth, which contains simple but extraordinarily powerful elements, available to every soul from this Planet. I understood this aspect after I became a Master in 7 spiritual systems, subsequently comprehending that our spiritual growth is based on the knowledge and the implementation of several simple elements known by every single one of us, on an inner, profound level. **These elements are** based on the knowledge which offers us access to health, happiness, wealth, beauty, harmony, love, forgiveness- to everything we could ever wish for in a lifetime. In consequence, I have proposed myself to perpetuate all my accumulated knowledge based on the basic elements mentioned above, to all of those who want to grow spiritually, but at the same time who want to live a better life.

If someone told you that a better life is available for any soul on this Planet- that we can access happiness, beauty and success through love, without a considerable effort, wouldn't that sound interesting? To see that your youth, glow and freshness are preserved? To magnetize, to awaken the admiration of those around you and why not, to leave something beautiful behind as you pass through life?

If the answer is YES, this means that the present book is in the hands of the right person, following the resonance principle. I have already started the transformation and I know that it is possible for us to receive all these. And if by transforming our lives in a good way, we are transforming Terra in a more beautiful planet for us and our children, or even for our future lives- then we most certainly haven't lived in vain!

If your answer is NO and you do not believe in the possibility of improving and transforming your life, then give this book as a gift to someone else: I am sure it will eventually get wherever it should...

And if you are not exactly sure how you can become a better person, if the past disappointments tired you and left you hopeless, I propose you to start a journey following these steps and, shortly after, enjoy the wonder which is starting NOW!

The magic wand will show its force through the 7 steps which I propose to start following from now on, in order to encompass them into our way of living. Soon enough the effects of a better health will be visible, as well as an inner and outer beauty, daily happy state of mind, wealth and harmony which will surround us!

And after you will start transforming your own lives, experiencing a certain support in everything you set your mind on doing, you will receive an inner blessing: fear of what is about to come disappears, the fog vanishes and you gain access to the beauty of life and you shall "awake" into the real life. You will learn how to truly communicate with those surrounding you, you will fell the warmth in the hearts of those who love you (they will be more and more), you will ditch the envy, jealousy, fear and you will let the stream of love, tenderness, inspiration, creativity, starting to taint others surrounding you making them want your presence...Then you realize you want to help them, to free those surrounding you, by receiving more blessing- because nothing helps a soul more than good deeds, that he gives and receives a reward countless times bigger...This is one of the Universal Laws: the fastest way of growth is helping other people, other souls which need to receive, in the same way in which we received while passing difficult periods in our life! I assure you that this way is fascinating, you shall never feel tired, bored, sick or tormented, because you won't need them anymore and the soul will grow without corrections, punishments, life lessons, which eventually have the role of awaking us…

No one can guarantee that there won't be any more lessons or challenges in the future, but you will certainly eliminate a great deal of your future problems, regarding health, accepting correction. Be sure that you will receive a lot of help and God will smile, proud of His children!

As a personal example, I got used to thank for the day which starts at the beginning of every day, for all the things I am going to learn, convinced that everything that comes to me is optimal for me. You should know it works, I am calm, serene, at peace and I easily accomplish whatever goal I set for myself. I have decided to bring into my life the magic wand, which I was telling you about and I am starting to see the beauty of life. I'm not saying life is easy, but I'm feeling more alive than ever…

At the end of every chapter I will introduce some practical advice zone, which represents the way in which these teachings can be implemented. To be more precise, everything you will have to do is to follow that advice. You will see that, soon enough, all these will be a part of your way of living, you will practice them in the subway, bus, while driving, before going to sleep, when you wake up, because they will transform your life into something you have always wished for but never knew how to achieve!

There is no other better moment to start something wonderful than NOW, let us start the journey together.

CHAPTER 1 - FORGIVENESS

Although at first sight this term seems to be connected to religion (which mentions it with great wisdom in the holly books), in reality it is a key to liberation from the energetic residues of the past, accumulated as a consequence of the sins and mistakes made by us or the ones who we interact with, towards the cure of our illnesses, towards the release of our mental and soul burdens.

Any physical disease which installs in the human body has its origin in an energetic disorder of an organ, coming as a consequence of sins, mistakes, defects, abuses or vices from previous years, all of these without any correction. After a while (which can be estimated in years, months or even days), when we have the opportunity to energetically correct whatever we are doing wrong, the disorder of the specific structure is transferred in the physical plan, generating an illness of a certain organ whose structure has been affected. But diseases may also appear as a consequence of some mistakes, guilt from the past, which must be cleansed in order not to generate problems in the future.

How can forgiveness help us in resolving these problems we are dealing with, in curing these illnesses which severely affect more and more persons?

Firstly we must understand the following mechanism, in other words "the mirror phenomena": everything that comes to as daily, is connected with whatever we "emit" to the outside world. Everything happens for a reason, the cause and effect law works at a universal level and cannot be changed by anyone. If we are selfish, envious, vengeful, it is only logical that the boomerang will come back to us, maybe at a time we least expect it to happen. The persons who we meet or with which we spend long periods of time, are the ones that we deserve as a consequence of our actions and attitude.

If in the moment something bad happens to us, an injustice is made or we simply suffer, we ask ourselves what is wrong with us and we ask ourselves what we did wrong. This is the first step in understanding the cause - effect mechanism which governs the universe. We must understand the fact that whatever we emit comes back to us sooner or later; that everything that burdens us and creates injustice, weighs down upon our future actions and consumes the energy of those actions.

You will ask now what can we do to neutralize the negative effect of these upsets, displeasures? We can use FORGIVENESS! When we forgive, the structures get clean, the energetic body is balanced, the "mist" which generates illnesses is lifted, nothing stands in the way of our actions anymore ...

This forgiveness mechanism represents a miracle recipe towards our inner peace, health, beauty and success.

It seems relevant to me to share the example of a person I know, who started suffering from a dermatological problem, which got complicated: any small scratch would rapidly transform into a swollen area, with blisters which spread on larger areas of the body; the treatment supposed admission to the hospital and administration of hydrocortisone. After his state got worst, the person in cause asked for the help of dermatologists and experts in the domain, who nodded their heads and associated the disease with blood circulation problems, with the nervous system and possibly the influence of varicosity, but did not find the curing remedy.

From a discussion with that person, he told me that previous to the disease, he had heard an agitated neighbor, in a moment of anger, talking badly about his children and he was so affected by these words that he promised himself to never forgive that woman; he even got to hate that woman for her words. After that he was too preoccupied with his health state to deal with his relationship with the neighbor.

During our discussions, I've come to the conclusion that no argument could convince him to forgive the neighbor who had talked badly of his children. Eventually it came to my mind and I told him, that he was free to live with and carry that burden, but he must be aware that everything unsolved in his lifetime (including this act of acknowledged unforgiving), will be transferred to his beloved children. At that moment I had his full attention; he then asked me what he could possibly do, I suggested to start by saying the prayer for forgiveness which I will mention at the end of this chapter (in the practical applications zone) addressed to his neighbor and to other persons with which he remembered having been upset with.

After a week, he told me that although in the beginning he did not believe in the power of those prayers, he rigorously said them in order to resolve his problems; he came to the point when he couldn't go to sleep without saying his prayers.

In an apparently surprising way, although the doctors recommended a surgery to relieve his blood circulation to cure his varicosity problem, there was no need for him to do that surgery because his health state got way better on its own.

After one month, there was no need for any medicine, his health condition was better than ever. I asked him without any pressure about his prayer saying and he answered smiling: "- I think I even forgave those who will wrong me in the future!"

Forgiveness is more than useful for all the therapists who work with patients, as a method of making the healing more efficient; when the therapist says the prayer prior to the therapy, he frees the communication channel with the patient, in order to help them latter. If surgeons nowadays would practice this cleansing method of the patient communicating channel, the surgery would go easier, eliminating some risks and complications…

As a matter of fact, the prayer for forgiveness is very useful prior to important discussions: at work, with your boss, before an interview, in negotiations, before meeting your beloved, before talking to your spouse or children. Practically, forgiveness cleans the energetic structures, healing faster and liberating the communication channels of older energetic residues, leading towards harmony and understanding.

How can we apply forgiveness with our entire soul, to escape from being sick and to build a better life? It seems easy to say, but very hard to get to… If we understand the fact that the persons who intentionally harm us are actually unhappy persons who need more our compassion than our revenge (which would imply "payments"), than it would be much easier for all of us! Only an unbalanced person, with great conduct problems or with serious health problems can act in an evil way on purpose! Therefore we can treat these persons carefully, with compassion, without any intention of mocking them or seeking revenge- this would mean we are fighting a man who is already dealing with serious problems…

I enjoyed a little story which I read in a magazine some time ago:

"A young woman was sitting and waiting for her flight in the waiting area of a big airport. And because she had to wait for some time, she bought a book and a pack of cookies, to help the time pass. She sat in the waiting room and started reading the book. She put her biscuits on the chair next to her and one seat further there was a man who was reading the newspaper. She opened the package of biscuits and after she ate the first biscuit, the person sitting next, took a biscuit too. She felt offended, but didn't say a word and continued reading the book. She was telling to herself <<look at this guy, if I only had more courage I would say something to him…>>

And each time she took a biscuit, he took one until one last biscuit remained in the package! She thought: <<I am curious to see what will he

say when there will be no more biscuits!>> The man took the last biscuit, split it into two pieces and gave her half of it. <<Oh, this can't be>>, thought the girl while taking her stuff, the book and the bag and walking towards the exit.

When she felt calmer, she sat on a chair in a more private corridor. She closed the book and opened her bag to put in the half biscuit she had received when... she sees her package of biscuits lying there untouched. She was ashamed by the way she acted and then realized that she had eaten the other person's cookies. The man shared with the girl even his last biscuit, without feeling offended, angry or superior."

The moral: How many times haven't we judged the ones surrounding us? How many times in our lives haven't we eat someone else's biscuits without realizing? Before getting to any conclusion and before thinking bad of someone, let us watch closely around us because usually things are different from what they appear to be!

There are 5 things in life which CANNOT BE RECOVERED:
- A stone, after you have thrown it;
- A word, after you said it;
- A chance, after you lost it;
- Time, after it has passed;
- Love, for the one who does not fight for it;

Forgiveness heals the already existing wounds of the soul and it works as a method of protection against all evil, and other types of energetic attacks: by saying the prayer for forgiveness addressed to a certain person, every negative projection coming from that person will go back to its initiator; as long as we are at peace with that specific person, an energetic shield is created to protect the positive thinker. He does not resonate with evil therefore he does not assimilate it. As much as we want to control everything that happens to us, we cannot, because we attract everything that we deserve, even if sometimes we are living under the impression that we have fooled others; the Laws of the Universe work after the energetic emissions and whatever bad deed we do, attracts pretty fast an equal lesson and vice-versa. The fact that we forgive and we are at peace with the ones surrounding us annuls the correction lessons. Even if apparently we are seeing something, in reality only the intention and the result are important in time, the more profound objective of an action, exemplified in the following joke:

"Jack and Max are walking out after the Sunday liturgy ends.
- You know, says Jack, I am accustomed to smoke while praying. Do you think that's ok?
- Why don't you ask the priest? Sais Max.
Jack goes and asks the priest:
- Father, can I smoke while praying?

- No son, this is not ok. It is a lack of respect for your faith.

Jack went back to his friend to share the priest's answer.

- No wonder he gave you this answer, you have asked the wrong question. Let me try.

- Father, can I pray while smoking?

- Of course my son!"

Our divine goal is to grow spiritually, to become better without suffering through the process. But at some times, suffering awakens us, it makes us easily realize our wrongs and it makes us react in a more rapid way towards correcting our faults. But by applying correction coming from ourselves, we are repaid by the light angels who are waiting for us to "awake" and understand our meaning on Earth.

SAYINGS ABOUT FORGIVENESS:

"Forgiveness is the fragrance that the violet sheds on the heel that has crushed it." **Mark Twain**

"It is easier to forgive an enemy, than to forgive a friend." **William Blake**

"The weak can never forgive. Forgiveness is the attribute of the strong." **Mohandas Gandhi**

"Forgive your enemies, but never forget their names." **John F. Kennedy**

"If there is something to pardon in everything, there is also something to condemn." **Friedrich Nietzsche**

PRACTICAL APPLICATIONS

And now let's get to work - we are practically starting, from now on, to cleanse our communication channels, our energetic structures and our entire organism, through forgiveness. What is there to do? Something very simple: each night, before going to bed, in a peaceful moment (after we have come at peace, by saying two prayers which I will mention in the followings), we must say from the bottom of our souls, with conviction, the prayer for forgiveness, after you have said the two preparative prayers "Heavenly Father" and "Mercifulness Door".

PREPARATIVE PRAYERS:

Heavenly Father

Heavenly father, consoler

The spirit of truth, present everywhere
You who accomplishes everything,
Treasurer of all good and life giver
Come lie within us
Cleanse all our evilness
And forgive our souls.
Amen!

Mercifulness door

Open for us the door to mercifulness
Blessed Virgin Mary, mother of God
For us, the ones who believe in you not to vanish
But to redeem of our needs through you,
For you are the redemption of the Christians.
Amen!

Prayer for forgiveness:

"**Jesus Christ, I ask for forgiveness with all my soul, and all my being to ...... (name) for all the harm that I have caused him/her in the past, I forgive ...... (name) for all the harm that he/she has caused me and I ask forgiveness to the Holy Trinity for all negative messages sent out in the Universe. Amen!**"

Throughout my experience I've come to the conclusion that these prayers, said for at least six times consecutively, can considerably amend the relationship with a certain person. If the whole process is so fast (only several minutes), don't you think the effort is worth it in order to lead a more beautiful, easier life???

Don't forget, the best moment to start is NOW.

CHAPTER 2 - HAPPINESS

During our daily life, we interact with many souls: from the one minute meetings on the elevator, to the ones spent with your life partner.

I woke up one morning with a state of happiness and inner peace, characterized by the lack of any burden. While I was walking to work, I asked myself why are we sometimes extremely happy when we feel the smell of coffee or when we hear the birds chirp, while other times our inner universe can be torn apart by a single thundery look; what is actually the key to a serene state of mind, in a material existence?

I was absorbed by my thoughts, while I noticed a lady sitting next to me in the elevator, who was looking at me very sad... the first thing which came into my mind was to say: "Good morning!" with a serene smile (which was rooted in my previous thoughts) on my face. I felt sympathy because I was happy and I wanted her to catch my state of mind, to encourage her to fight for her own good, for a more beautiful life! She replied confused and a little bit irritated and then got out of the elevator with an uncertain smile...

I had seen again that lady a couple of days later and I noticed that her face lit up when seeing me- I understood that we had communicated from soul to soul...

I tried understanding the mechanism and realized that the state of happiness comes from our inner conciliation, from the unburdening (through forgiveness) of other people's mistakes, from lifting ourselves above the impulse of seeking revenge, from the love and kindness deeds regarding any known or apparently stranger soul. A noble feeling emerges and it obliges us to accede to a superior level, we cannot go down again because we want that terrific state of mind do be there forever... Moreover, happiness is contagious! By surrounding yourself with happy people, you will learn to smile, to give...to love- because happiness is based on the capacity to love.

American researchers did a study regarding the smile and came to the conclusion that people who are most successful in any domain (even those which imply maximum seriousness), are the ones who smile; these people are rarely left by their life partner, they are never fired from a job, they attract success through high-spirits! Who wouldn't want to be surrounded by joyful people, well intended and positive? By doing this you become irreplaceable for the people surrounding you, they will all await for you with pleasure and through this way you shall attract success, including the material success, but more important, that "spiritual gold" which is actually the good luck we all appeal to when we need it.

To parenthesize, all our good deeds, done because someone asked us to or done unconditionally, are accumulated under the form of good energy, which is spilled when we need it to, in order for us to grow. This is why they say that good luck isn't random; it actually is the result of our previous deeds. If we accumulate luck (spiritual gold) through good deeds done for people we know or for apparent strangers (I am saying "apparent strangers" because in reality a stranger can be a soul with which we might have interacted somewhere, somehow), we can use this potential when a special moment appears in our life, through prayer to God; or we can pray that "God's will be done concerning my optimal way". I am using this latter version, because I might pray for a growth of the money gain, while optimal for me would be the apparition of a great love- God knows best what I need in order to get to the highest point of my spiritual growth!

Going back to the smile, what could we do to become more appealing, to magnetize and to attract success? We can start NOW, when we get up in the morning, to smile at thinking that we exist in this world through God's Will, that He brought us here to experience life, that He loves us all as His children and that He sends us exactly what we need to grow us.

Smile for this day, which brings to you exactly what you need to achieve progress, to identify the people which can support you through this journey, smile to life and life will smile back to you !

Do you know the beauty of this exercise? That shortly, maybe in the same day, the "answers" will come along: people will be surprised by you, knowing what you were like before, they will start liking the new you more and more, you shall become more beautiful and your luck will repay you, for you enlighten so many souls with your attitude! Effects are only positive, I can guarantee: you will magnetize, you will be prettier, you will attract success and life will smile back to you!

Maybe you have read about "the secret" promoted in some books, which has existed forever, as a law of the Universe: you receive whatever you emit in the outside world. You are preoccupied by thoughts regarding illness? Shortly after, the Universe accumulates the answer through the vibration which you emit generating health problems. You are preoccupied by thoughts regarding love and positive communication with those surrounding you? Shortly after this the ones who you interact with will look for you, will love you and will be attracted by you! It's simple!

I liked this little story which I noticed on the internet:

"A dog walked into a room made only out of mirrors; it looked around and suddenly saw a pack of dogs surrounding and looking at it.

Not knowing what to do, it thought that by growling it would scare everyone away. It did this and suddenly all the dogs growled back threatening it; it then thought it must attack first, other ways it stood no chance to defeat them. It then attacked the mirror hitting his head against it and dying.

The moral: what would have happened to this dog if it had friendly wagged his tail???"

Life is pretty much the same: if at first sight we check out people suspiciously, expecting only negative intentions coming from them, we will get the same treatment. If we start a discussion with a smile, showing our inner light, nobody will resist and you shall be able to see the positive effects shortly after.

The smile must be learnt, trained, not everyone is born with the pleasure of smiling... you can start by thinking about a time when you were happy: the thought of when you have fallen in love, or the thought of when you saw your first born, something beautiful which brought warmth into your soul. Using that positive energy, smile from the inside, with light on your face, imagining the great moments you will experience in the future- those are answers for your smile to life, to the Universe, which always work!

After you get used to smile from the inside do it as often as you can: think of the fact that there are people with greater burdens than yours, who don't have access to all this information. Smile gently, with warmth to them, they'll feel better, encourage them to hope and you will accumulate that pure spiritual gold received for every good deed! We have nothing to lose by being good, actually our life transforms in a better one, we become more beautiful, brighter and, why not, wealthier both material and spiritual... God loves us all, there is place for all of us on earth, we must only ask for what is ours and we must be able to offer our help to others in order to receive it when we need it!

After we have learnt this mechanism, our inner well-being won't allow us to descend towards feelings like envy, revenge, aggressiveness. We will embrace good and it will be visible in every aspect of our life: in our relationship with our life partner (who will fall in love again with your inner and outer beauty), in your success at work, in money gain and also in our state of happiness, which will be transformed miraculously!

I was talking to a friend and he was telling me that he couldn't entirely be glad of a good certain thing in his life because he was constantly thinking that each joy in life is followed by sorrow, in order to "rebalance" the situation. Actually, the message sent to the Universe is, in this case, that something bad must happen creating a negative condition which eventually happens, if someone "asks for it". My advice is to allow ourselves sincere happiness each time we have the occasion, without fearing or feeling guilty because we are happy, attracting in this way and spreading the feeling of happiness. It is our right to feed our soul with every occasion, in this way we can actually cast away negative happenings, thanks to the emitted optimism... Negative energies (illnesses, negative thoughts, limitations) reject optimism, because it provides tremendous amounts of light, God is present therefore there is no place for negativity. Why shouldn't we prolong this positive effect, by convincing ourselves that we deserve to experience these moments; moreover we must try to help as many people as we can to experience this inner state of happiness, which implies health, harmony, success in whatever we want to do.

I have been applying a philosophy for 9-10 years, since I have started my spiritual searches, trying to understand the world and this passage of mine through life: each existence is like a part we play, which helps us to experience knowledge of the outer world and, most of the time, even our self-knowledge. It helps us to find OUR INNER-SELVES, love our mistakes because they bring knowledge, learning to explore. If we find ourselves here and now, let's play this "game" the right way, let's not waste time, cherishing it. If I am going to work, I want to do it as good as I can, to leave a trace behind. If I am raising a child, I want to make him/her glad because he/she "chose" me as his/her parent in this existence (many theories state the fact that children coose us as parents, we aren't the ones to decide). If I have a man by my side, I must help him come home to a pleasant environment, experience a good state of mind, understanding that I am not the leader. I am learning to open my eyes wide upon my life, I am learning to make decisions without fear and I dream about the beautiful moments which I am certain will come. I free myself from prejudice and the fear of tomorrow, making place for hope and belief in the day that will come, waiting anxiously for whatever awaits me in the future... Only then you shall actually see how blue the sky is, the color of the leafs in the beginning of the fall, you will have time to enjoy a child's smile, you will be able to look into the eyes which have been loving you for years and which you have neglected for so long because of your burdens, you will see parts of life which you won't believe existed. Anyway, by worrying you will not solve your problems and sadness will not clarify any incertitude, let's live our "role" as beautiful as we can, let's have fun while passing through experiences, let's treat others with more attention , let's awake for the rest of our lives. I know, you'll say (this was too my way of answering) it is easy to say that you wish for a better life, but there are illnesses which do not allow us, there are grandchildren who need to be raised so that we could help our children who are overwhelmed by worries, there are debts which do not allow us to sleep well at night!

Let me tell you a big secret: all these come as an answer to the nightmare we are living on an inner level. Let's regard our life as a role to the end of which we must propose to gain an Oscar prize! Almost any illness can be cast away by changing our state of mind entirely, hoping with every breath we take, sharing unconditional love! Illnesses are negative energies casted away by love, optimism, gentleness, their freedom ends where there is light! We are actually feeding them with black thoughts and abandonment when facing difficulties... If we are playing our "role", let's accept with dignity whatever it has to offer, let's love as much as we can, let's help by saying a good word to a person in need, let's make of our past a beautiful image to look upon and let's look towards the future with hope!

I can assure you a very beautiful effect will appear during this transformation: that will make you proud of what you've become; you shall assure a type of beauty which does not include age or cosmetic products!

SAYINGS ABOUT HAPPINESS:

"Men's happiness or misery is most part of their own making." **John Locke**

"To love means to suffer;to be happy is to love. So to be happy means to suffer, but suffering makes one unhappy. Therefore, to be happy, one must love or love to suffer or suffer from too much happiness." Woody Allen

"There are people incapable of tasting happiness. For them, this happiness is only a cold word, written in a dictionary." **Emil Cioran**

"I have learned that everybody wants to live at the top of the mountain, forgetting that how we climb is all that matters." **Gabriel Garcia Marquez**

"We have no more right to consume happiness without producing it than to consume wealth without producing it." **George Bernard Shaw**

PRACTICAL APPLICATIONS:

I suggest you start your actions by saying the prayers mentioned in the previous chapter: Heavenly Father and Mercifulness Door, for a prior cleansing of our structures and for a peaceful mind, for assuring maximum efficiency in our endeavor.

In this chapter, I suggest you say each morning when you wake up or before going to sleep at night the following prayer which introduces exactly the situations you need, the interactions which can make your life easier and which can attract whatever it is that you need to become happier and more confident:

"Jesus Christ, Son of God, I thank you for the day that is about to begin for me, for the circumstances and optimal interactions, for fulfilling my mission and my personal growth, I thank you for the help you are sending me on every level, in order to have the power to fulfill my path and find my inner peace, I thank you for the love I'm receiving and spreading, for accepting to manifest through me! Amen!"

You will see how your path gets smoother, how the perfect situations come to you and the persons you need in order to evolve help you to achieve your goals easier.

I have made a comparison, during a short period of time (several days) I stopped saying any kind of prayer in the morning and it was like everything was chaotic: projects which were about to be finalized got mixed up, I found myself in the middle of some conflicts which stopped my initiative- shortly, everything was out of control... by using the prayer specified above, you will feel how your path gets smoother and you get to achieve your goals with minimum efforts!

Let's start together, right NOW. Why shouldn't we simplify our life, both from home and from the places where we work?

The "secret" known by all the great spiritual masters, seemed fascinating to me. I've read it in a book written by an American guywho lived for many years in Tibet, among very clean spiritual people, who teleported themselves, levitated and traveled throughout the entire Universe... The perfect prayer, which is never refused by God because it follows another Universal law, is the one through which we give thanks to God for whatever we are wishing for! Our faith in Him is repaid; we are receiving exactly what we are wishing for, if our wishes do not imply harming others! For example if I wish to receive the gift of kindness, I thank God for my kindness, for being calmer, more at peace with myself and this gift shall come soon... We only have to be grateful from the depths of our soul and be convinced that we shall receive whatever we are asking for. I have applied this method and I can assure you it works! And you can use it in any domain, it has the same efficiency!

CHAPTER 3 - LOVE

The love which we lay upon people is like a light which discovers things lying in the dark. Through love, we know and see the other person in his/her true light. Only love can truly see. If someone wants to know what to see with your Spirit means, he/she must know that LOVE is the answer. When loving someone, you wish to do as he/she wishes, right to the point where your thoughts identify with his/her thoughts, you start experiencing him/her in your own heart, in your own body, in your own breath, all these happen at a level where the one you love reveals him/herself, as a whole, in yourself, as yourself." (Ieromonarh Salvatie Bastovoi)

Have you ever seen a person who was in love? Most certainly it has happened to you too at least once in a lifetime and you can probably remember the zealousness from your soul, that happy, floating state, when the person becomes more beautiful, more inspired, luckier, more... All this wellness is explained through the interior harmony of a person who loves, the highest form of energy is released, all the energetic centers are nourished and a rejuvenation of the entire structure takes place - this is how love works. Through love, the body gets healthier, it balances and it accumulates a type of good energy, which produces a very favorable, energetic jump.

Practically, when we fell in love we are getting close to that vibration level which we cannot maintain without capturing and reflecting love through the mechanism I will later present.

If we could maintain the effects of love for a longer period of time, maybe for a few years, we would most certainly grow a lot faster, we wouldn't get sick anymore, we would become more beautiful and we would get to keep our youth longer, receiving that aura which attracts and magnetizes. But in many cases, the person who we fall in love with disappoints us, therefore we go back to that dull energetic state, full of disbelief and lacking courage, without the power of moving things to our favor.

What is there to do?

Firstly, we have to learn to receive and spread the love, to captivate those energies which come out of love from the entire Universe and then we must spread that huge force all around us, to people, plants, animals, places, situations. What happens exactly? We will not spread our energy (we don't poses that amount of energy), but we will channel the love energy from the Universe (the light of God) which we can capture through our capacity, towards everything we encounter.

This process is not a complex one, we must only ask ourselves to reflect love, to become the manifestation of God on earth ("God is love") and those effects I was talking about earlier become visible:

- The level of our vibration grows, protecting us from illnesses and from other dangers;

- We manifest ourselves as God's children, in His image, spreading light and love on earth;

- We become younger, more beautiful;

- We reflect light and love, people will feel good around us, recharged;

- Our divine right increases, we accumulate "spiritual gold" which generates our right to be happy, to receive material rights and spiritual gifts;

By accepting to become God's messengers on earth, to reflect love, we are maintaining the coordinates specific to the in love state, which gives us access to the highest energetic form.

Probably you have heard or read about the notion of **soul mates**, which generates the perfect harmony between two souls, forming that balance through merger. Meeting a soul mate may never occur, even if both souls are seeking each other without knowing, but when it occurs it comes simple, as a natural compatibility, with no efforts, through a powerful sensation of completeness.

Specifically because this kind of love offers an enormous chance to manifest God, it comes after many efforts and acceptance, after suffering and forgiving, after reaching a level challenged by growth and balance… And then, LOVE must be acknowledged and respected, even if it shows up when we least expected it, when we are overwhelmed by the daily routine, when we are mostly discouraged by the disbelief of ever knowing how it feels… Once acknowledged, the love for the soul mate must be lived accordingly to its greatness, knowing that you have been blessed by God!

The most lasting couples are those who manifest God. Both partners are aware of the fact that they met thanks to the Divine Will, when they are grateful for what they have received, when they can enjoy together the transformations within their relationship and when they have the capacity to reflect love to the outside. When a couple prays together, their relationship solders, they are blessed and defended, the partners grow together.

All our good deeds done throughout a lifetime help us access that certain spiritual level which facilitates the encounter with our soul mate, or with the optimal partner for us.

If sometime, in the past, we've refused love by playing with someone else's feelings, it is much harder to meet our soul mate until we right our past wrongs.

There are cases in which we feel a very powerful attraction towards a person of the opposite sex, situation which may end up in marriage (we feel unaware of anyone else's existence but the person in cause), although we do not feel in the seventh heaven; these cases may indicate an "apparent love", which most of the time ends up in divorce/rupture. In these cases, we are talking about a very big karmic debt between the two (one, the other or both generated suffering for the other somehow) and they feel soul attraction in order to repair their past mistakes. When the mistakes are reclaimed and the balance is set again, they suddenly awake. In conformity with their actual feelings, they can choose to continue their path together, developing the real love, or to separate and start searching for their real soul mate, which they were not entitled to know because of previous mistakes.

I saw a couple several years ago who used to argue permanently and who made life impossible for each other, but when they decided to separate, they realized they couldn't be apart from each other. It was like they needed interaction, although there was no harmony between them; I've made measurements through divining methods and came to the conclusion that the two had a very powerful karmic relationship. They needed to forgive each other for the pain caused in the past, therefore they punished each other each time they had an occasion. That was not love it was more of a powerful need for forgiveness which could transform itself into love, if the two of them could get over their own egos.

This is why it helps if, at the beginning of a relationship, we say our prayers for forgiveness with our partner and with his family, in order to help build a strong relationship and to generate chances for the couple.

I've seen cases when the close relatives of one partner had karmic relationships (debts from the past) with the other partner, they were tempted to come between the couple's relationship. These cases are the most known, with in-laws capable of crazy things to stop the union of their children (famous examples throughout classical literature: Romeo and Juliet, Tristan and Isolde, they all faced tragic situations because of the hatred manifested between their families). These cases were more tragic as the two matching souls had found each other!

It is known that once you've found your soul mate, nobody else seems appealing anymore, harmony appears and the match is so intense that no other feeling can rise at that level.

To parenthesize, women who had miscarriages and especially those who had more than two abortions must know that those rejected souls are "trapped" in an intermediary zone (between the worlds) without any chance of growth. The mother who got rid of them is directly responsible for helping them go towards the light, in Heaven. Normally, whatever that mother accumulates spiritually goes straight to those souls, in order to help them reach the light. That's why there are women, who do enough good deeds, but their life is not improving and they do not understand why.

In the case in which we are dealing with several abortions, the woman who did them has accumulated many serious sins (abortions are sins against the Holy Spirit) and that is why they can generate serious illnesses, even death if the good deeds in compensation are insufficient or if there is no significant spiritual growth, so that it could cover the necessity of those souls to reach the light. Written below, in the practical application zone, I'll tell you how to help those rejected souls, aborted, to go into the light, so that you could grow and live a better life.

I need to mention the fact that in case of an abortion, the father is also responsible, because he did not try to help that soul seing the light, because he did not help the mother create the conditions for raising the soul. I recommend that men who know that their wife/life partner/lover had at least one abortion, to follow these advice, in order to liberate themselves energetically from the bind which is stopping their growth and their well-being.

Going back to love and its manifestations, our growth through love is produced more intense and profound as we succeed to free ourselves of conditionings, of limitations. For example, if we want the optimal man/woman for us to appear but in parallel we want he/she to have a degree of prosperity which generates material relaxation, then we are knowingly limiting or postponing the moment of encounter, through our disbelief in the Divine Will, by setting conditions which further us away from our path. We must trust that if the encounter takes place, he/she will have the necessary coordinates for us to be satisfied and grow together. And when we love unconditionally, money will appear, the house will come, understanding will be present- practically it all is like a blank check we offer to God, trusting His judgment. How do we recognize the optimal man/woman for us? We will feel the compatibility, the easiness in loving that soul, something dear to us coming from our soul...

I really liked a little story which truly represents a love lesson: "Moses Mendelssohn, the grandfather of the well known German composer, was a man far from being handsome. Contrariwise, apart from the fact that he was not tall at all, he also had a grotesque hunchback. One day he visited a merchant from Hamburg, who had a very pretty girl, named Frumtje.

Moses fell madly in love with the girl who looked at him with repulsion. When he visited the merchant's house, before leaving, Moses gathered some courage, went to the first floor, where the girl's room was so that he could have a few words with her before leaving. She was heavenly beautiful and he felt tortured by the fact that she would refuse to at least look at him. After several attempts to start a conversation, Moses asked her with a shy voice: "Do you know why marriages are done in Heaven?" "Yes", answered the girl, while she was facing the floor. "But do you know why?" "Yes, I know", answered him. "You see, in Heaven, at the birth of every boy, God announces that he would marry a girl. When I was born, I was shown my bride to be. The Lord told me: your bride will be a hunchback. I told Him then: "My Lord, a woman with a hunchback would be a tragedy. Give me the hunchback and let her be beautiful."

Fascinated by his words, Frumtje lifted her sight from the floor, and later agreed to become that man's faithful wife."

You'll ask how we can find out when something or someone is our destiny, if we are compatible or if it must be part of our path…

The answer is: when our soul opens, when we feel a great joy from the inside! If you want to buy a car, the optimal choice is when you feel happiness in your heart, when you feel that the gates are opening. In the same way, when we get hired, if we experience a burden it means that that place is not part of our path… we must learn to listen to our soul, it is the "compass" in our choices, regardless if it is about choosing a pair of shoes or choosing the partner you wish to have by your side the rest of your life!

The reason lies in the fact that the soul is part of God, the Divine spark received by us at birth as being our cleanest part, in which we must invest trust. The moment we become more balanced, powerful and in harmony with our being, that is when we start listening to our soul.

SAYINGS ABOUT LOVE:

"If I knew that today would be the last time I'd see you, I would hug you tight and pray the Lord be the keeper of your soul. If I knew that this would be the last time you pass through this door, I'd embrace you, kiss you, and call you back for one more. If I knew that this would be the last time I would hear your voice, I'd take hold of each word to be able to hear it over and over again. If I knew this is the last time I see you, I'd tell you I love you, and would not just assume foolishly you know it already." **Gabriel Garcia Marquez**

"It is better to have loved and lost than never to have loved at all." **Lord Alfred Tennyson**

"The more one judges, the less one loves." **Honore de Balzac**

"Love is patient, love is good and it does not envy anyone. Love is not boastful, nor self-sufficient or rude; never selfish and it cannot be humiliated. Love can conquer anything, there are no limits for her faith and love is hope and patience. In one word, there are three things which will always exist: faith, hope and love; but the greatest of them is love. " **Bible**

What are we going to do to manifest and spread the love on earth, in order to attract growth, prosperity and wellness?

PRACTICAL APPLICATIONS

What I am about to explain below is a very simple procedure, which can be done in any moment of a day, during a discussion, in the subway, in the tram, in the car or even when meeting with your friends.

To parenthesize, I have found out through different attempts in the past years, that everything we are imagining determines the future and, why not, the present. I mean, if we visualize in our mind (with as many details as possible)that a certain action takes place, this is most likely to happen, because it comes through that anticipated faith according to which God offers us whatever we want, if we do not harm others with this action. For example you want a certain car and for rushing the process, you will imagine the moment in which you are actually buying it, with the excitement you feel when driving it for the first time, with the details about the color, type…

Accordingly with your trust in these beliefs, the ways to transforming them into reality will appear. In the same way, as an example, if you made a mistake and you've hurt someone badly, firstly you can imagine the real side of the story, which happened and then you can replace it with the story you wish to implement, the ideal one. The negative energies generated by the action you wish to avoid, will be cured.

All right, then we have established that this exercise of imagination is helpful for obtaining what we want. Let's go back to love and its manifestation –you can imagine a pink-green light (colors radiated by the chakras in the moment we feel love) which comes from above and passes through your heart chakra, and which you spread towards people from one room, town, plants, landscapes from a journey, towards surroundings, situations or moments. You will observe how everything resolves itself calmly, people become more cooperative, more harmonious and things get balanced in a good way for yourself.

Moreover, you'll feel an inner balance, calmness, and power, from the first month since you start practicing, you will transform. It isn't hard and you'll become love's messenger on earth, your soul will open and you shall see soon the positive effects in your life!

I've promised a prayer which I recommend to all of those who have decided to make an abortion. I suggest you to say it daily, until you feel liberated from thinking of those little souls. I suggest you, as a mother to seek help also coming from your priest, because the light will get to those little souls in this way.

Prayer for the aborted souls

"I am blessing with the love of God the souls of my aborted children, I ask for their forgiveness from the bottom of my soul because I have rejected them and I ask forgiveness from the Holy Trinity for all the evil that I emitted in the Universe. I am asking our Savior Jesus Christ and Virgin Mary to help these souls rise into the light, accordingly to the Divine Will. Amen! "

Below I have written a prayer for love, in order for you to find the suitable person, the optimal soul to love and to offer your love. May God help us!

Prayer for love/the loved person

"God I wish for a man/a woman, to get along with, to be my confident; I wish so much for a person, to love and to love me back! Help me God, to meet someone suitable for me, someone with serious intentions, a life partner. I want to love, to make someone happy! Watch over me, Lord and give me the power and the longevity of your love and protect me forever! Amen!"

CLAUDIA NITA DONCA

CHAPTER 4 - ABUNDANCE / WEALTH

This chapter will come as a surprise for many of you, because we are used to limit ourselves regarding gain, wealth, money, considering that we are not entitled to a well-being over the average. We think that only people with a special social status have access to wealth, accepting from the beginning some kind of resignation in this direction. Some of us even consider that it is wrong to pray for money and wealth, because this aspect is inferior to other aspects regarding the soul.

Well, this specific resignation attitude makes us emit in the Universe, the thought that we don't need money. And according to the Universal Law which states that we get what we emit, our actions will generate the lack of wealth, of money.

To understand better, a grand master from Russia, a therapist with great spiritual force, was asked by a lady what is the correct way to act: as a saint who turns the other cheek when he gets hit, or as a entrepreneur who uses any occasion to make money? And the answer was: "As an entrepreneur saint!"

This means we are allowed to gain wealth and money, if we abide by the laws of the Universe; there are light entities, gain angels which guide us into the path which leads us to a state of abundance correlated with our **divine right to money**, meaning if we deserve this financial abundance, which can come to us as an income/salary, car, house, the right to travel, the right of having a certain social status. Of course, a person's divine right to money has to do with:

- The number of good deeds done by that soul;
- How anchored that soul is in the material world- a person who would step on other people to obtain financial success, is unbalanced in this area and he cannot receive what will further unbalance him;
- The person's credits regarding his peers: a correct attitude, moral,

without affecting other souls;

- Very important: the existence of a preoccupation (without becoming an obsession) of "making money"; I've met several cases in which people are complaining that they have no money, without thinking, cooperating or searching for a way to get more money;

- The way in which, by generating an excess of money, we would help other souls to progress on their path: nothing accelerates more the appearance of the gain than the fact that that money is going to be used in a way which implies our and others souls growth (example: a school, a kindergarten, a foundation for helping the elders, all these would influence in a positive way other souls).

Nowadays, business men make charity actions in order to maintain their divine right in money. They allocate a percentage of their turnover for this kind of action. Maybe you have heard the term "tenth" which represents an old biblical tradition, through which 10% of whatever we are gaining, must be used to help others.

- The way in which we are using the money gain: if a person which has a big income uses the money for his personal fun, wasting that income without growing in some way, he loses that divine right to money and starts losing money;

- The way in which we are sending love when we have more money: if we are crushing others with our new status, it doesn't help us; if we manifest understanding, love, morality, we will surely obtain greater rights;

God wants us all to be happy and he gives us the right, because we are His children. We are allowed to receive whatever we want, under one condition: that what we want mustn't contravene with the Laws of the Universe, meaning we mustn't hurt other souls, we must manifest love, accept that what we emit comes back to us, to avoid anchoring in order to be able to maintain our soul's balance, to do as many good deeds as we can, to be wise and loving.

Financial abundance is manifested on Earth only, in the physical plan of material existence; in the soul's reality, there are other criteria which make us happy: the power of loving, of being loved, the power of doing good deeds, the power of forgiving, of manifesting compassion and understanding, of being good and loving. And if by doing all these, we also want to access wealth, there is nothing wrong, we have a divine right in money, which can be measured!

I remember the time when, after 7 years of working in a company where I was constantly growing and where every single one of my projects was part of me, I suddenly felt many injustices coming to me and it was like the situation had become impossible there, although the level of my salary and of the respect shown to me were satisfying. I couldn't understand why all of a sudden things were happening so that I could leave. After tormenting myself for several weeks, I suddenly found out about an offer from another company, a lot more financial potent, for a better job than the previous one. I've applied for that job so that I could verify my potential, but as the situation at the existent job was getting worst, I decided to accept the new offer with confidence.

Now, looking into the past, I realize that my divine right to money had grown, fact of which I wasn't aware at that time. Although I asked myself for several weeks what I was doing wrong to experience all that, in reality I was pushed towards a more wealthy gain!

My dears, this is the beauty of life, nothing is what it seems!!! We sometimes receive AWARDS which we perceive as challenges or problems and other times we believe that we are making our life easier when actually we are slipping on the slope of attachments which generate unbalance... nothing is more beautiful for a woman than to give birth to a child and sadly we sometimes perceive this special moment as a mistake, we reject it and we make mistakes which we carry around for a long time. Other times we receive LOVE through encountering the person we fall in love with and sometimes we say to ourselves "I want a carrier, then I allow myself to fall in love", other times we receive wealth through a big income, forgetting to live with our heart- there are many situations in which we misinterpret what is happening to us and we make mistakes!

All these feelings that we are living appear so that we could realize together that as long as we follow the right track, manifesting love, forgiveness, compassion, kindness but also intelligence, wisdom, adapted to our days, there are no limits in obtaining whatever we want!

Because by manifesting these gifts, we do not want to act against other people in the Universe!!!

There is a funny story about "two friends who met in a bar, to have a coffee. Depressed, one of them started to tell the other about his preoccupations...work...money...his relationship with his girlfriend...his life goals... Everything seemed to go bad for him. The other one slipped his hand into his pocked, and picked a 50 euro bill and said:

- Do you want this bill?

- Of course... it's 50 euro, who wouldn't want it? The one who had the bill crumpled it in his hand.

- Now, do you still want it?

- It's still 50 euro. Of course I want it, if you give it to me. The friend threw the bill on the floor and stepped on it, until it got all dirty.

- Do you still want the bill?

- It is still a 50 euro bill even if you pull it apart it's still valuable...

- Do you see now? You must know, that even if sometimes things don't go as you wish, even if life crumples you,you continue being as important as you always were... What needs to be corrected is your real worth regarding the problems you have at a certain moment. Then he put the bill next to him on the table and said with a smile on his face:

- Take it, keep it so you remember this moment when you're feeling down... but you must give me a new 50 euro bill so that I could use it with the next friend in need..."

There is one more aspect which you've surely heard of in other discussions, but in which not everybody believes, because it cannot be seen- I am talking about KARMA. Even if it is or it isn't important that we have lived assuming actions which generate consequences on long term, it is a fact that we come into this world with an ancestral load through which we receive in this life some challenges, some lessons, which, if we act correctly, can correct this informational load carried by our soul. It is only normal that if we have previous sins concerning money, we must first correct those mistakes in order to obtain the wanted wealth. But because we don't always know which our challenges are, we can make these aspects easier through a proper conduct, assumed from NOW on!

To be more precise, it is possible to see persons around you who are presently doing good deeds and act correctly from a moral point of view, but who are going through tough times for which we pity them, considering that life's not fair... In reality, this is our perception, subjective, without knowing what mistakes has that soul committed and with what karmic baggage it came in this life; if he tormented other souls and if he provoked unhappiness around, he has chosen these challenges before being born, specifically for cleaning his past mistakes. If during these attempts, that soul acts correctly ant he assumes the lessons which he himself choose before being born as objectives, he progresses enormously and shall receive countless rewards. God is fair with everyone, we are all His children and He loves us equally, being proud of our moments of growth; but He allows certain lessons because He respects our free will assumed by us before birth as the objectives of our evolution and to correct what we did wrong in the past.

I had riot moments in the past, when I saw cases where the victim was absolutely innocent (a child or a very moral and gentle person), considering unfair that good people suffer and those who do bad to triumph. I understood later, by reading and feeling that actually those souls were passing over their lessons, while those who were doing bad also received the lessons for which they were punished too, so that they could grow, understand correctly that by doing bad deeds you cannot receive good in return.

To parenthesize, I am going to tell you about an interesting case which took place when I was taking courses and learning reiki therapies; one day, while being at the office, I found out where I was working at that time, and I was occupying a marketing position, that a colleague of mine was passing through a real tragedy: while transporting their luggage from their car to the hotel room, in Bulgaria, his 2 year old boy was looking at his father he slipped off the balcony, fell and died instantly. That night, I couldn't close an eye, thinking to the tragedy the two parents were going through. I contacted my colleague, with whom I hadn't interacted before and told him that I was constantly dreaming about a child who is asking me to help the two unhappy parents, who were harming him through their despair. I took them to a psychic, who managed to "see" what had happened: the child's parents had heavy karma, sins which hovered over them and their family and this child had proposed to himself as a personal mission to take his parents sins away, through his suffering, in order to help them to grow faster. By setting them free of their sins, they would have been able to give birth to a healthy child, creating greater chances of growth for the entire family. So it happened, the next year another boy was born in that family, in the same day as the child who was no longer here. Later I found out that, the child had asked for help in my dreams because he once was my father, so that's why he could communicate with me.

It is interesting how things aren't what they appear to be, but sometimes it is very hard to access the wisdom needed in order to accept them... we can, in exchange to trust The one Above, which acts for the greater good for every single soul!

Going back to the gain, if we want money, material values, wealth and financial abundance, we must be those **entrepreneur saints** which I was telling you about earlier, we must leave envy behind, act intelligently, with compassion, with forgiveness and wisdom and we mustn't waste our time judging others (because we do not poses all the coordinates which could give us a right angle for judging what seems just or unjust) and surround ourselves with people who share our moral values, in order to find our perfect environment, like the fish in the water! **The presence of the person we love, in our life is very important**, the "soul mate" with whom we build the optimal team for this lifetime, with whom we have children and who allows us to see a meaning in everything, by manifesting God in all our actions!

SAYINGS ABOUT MONEY:

"Money is like a sixth sense without which you cannot make a complete use of the other five." **Somerset Maugham**

"Time is more valuable than money. You can get more money, but you cannot get more time." **Jim Rohn**

"The life of money-making is one undertaken under compulsion and wealth is evidently not the good we are seeking for it is merely useful and for the sake of something else." **ARISTOTLE**

PRACTICAL APPLICATIONS

I believe that every person has the right to ask, through prayer, to access the divine right to money which he/she deserves and I have seen many persons who are way below this level because they do not acknowledge the way in which they could get more and they don't do anything in this direction.

Prayer for money:

"Jesus Christ, Son of God, I thank you for what I have and for your help in obtaining the money gain which I deserve thanks to the divine right! Untie, God, with your light and power, my money gain, of any aggressions did against my free will and give me God wealth, happiness and gain, to fulfill in an optimal way my life mission! I thank You God for the abundance and the gain in money and help me God to do with it whatever suits my path! Amen. "

It is possible for the light angels who deal with our money gain to be tied down through our past wrong actions (we were greedy and gained great sums of money without deserving it). By saying faithfully each night the previous prayer, with gratitude for what we have and for what we are convinced we are about to receive, the energies opposed to our divine right will be eliminated.

May God help us!

CHAPTER 5 - BEAUTY

This chapter is a very interesting one, because it will surprise many of those who have/had preconceptions about beauty. There are so many young ladies or ladies (men rely mostly on other characteristics in order to be successful, although beauty is important for us all) convinced that they haven't got weapons to "fight", and that nature hasn't gifted them enough from the beginning, that the fight is already lost...

I come now to bring you peace and to tell you that we can be charming, we can become the loved woman for the man of our dreams, we can be successful and lead a fulfilled life, if we understand a little bit of the "wisdom" of beauty! This also applies to men.

Do you remember what I was telling you about earlier? About the spiritual gold which accumulates as we do good deeds? This spiritual gold, this love and good deeds accumulation, generates a very interesting mechanism: it attracts light entities (we can call them angels) which are responsible for love, health, wealth, harmony but also for the inner and outer beauty.

These angels can't wait to "have work to do" in order to find souls which are willing to grow, to become better with those surrounding them. So these angels come to help and repay these people (man and women). I cannot describe a man who is going through this kind of transformation, a man who chooses the way of love, kindness, of the attempt to grow, of doing the right things at least from NOW ON in the light of God. That person is actually earning his right to be more beautiful, both on an inner and on an outer level, the right to love and being loved, the right to have money and success!!! Try for at least one month to apply these teachings and you shall see HOW you'll transform, you'll see how people will feel magnetized by you and will be amazed of you never getting old, in contrary, your sight will earn a certain glow, your body will become more harmonious and you shall be lucky even though you don't really ask for that!

To parenthesize, I remember my dreams as a child, when I wanted very badly to be beautiful and I was telling everyone that I was going to become a bride, wear a long dress and be elegant. Honestly, I was a child like so many others and my dreams were all about beauty! At about 20 years old, I was a pretty profound young girl, preoccupied of understanding people, but now, looking back, I can say that the real beauty did not "come" when I dreamt about it or when I was expecting it, but far more later, when I've learned that I must take care of my soul, to nurture and raise it- and that was the time the light that generates exterior and inner beauty started to appear.

It is very interesting that we mustn't do great efforts to become more beautiful, if we apply the teachings which help us clean our interior! I warn you that everybody will ask you what recipe are you using, what gym are you going to, which products are you using, why are you getting younger with the passage of time…

Inner beauty comes out of harmony, kindness, love, and totally understanding the phenomena which states that you needn't fight anyone in order to grow: as long as you are helping another soul to grow (through thought, word/advice, deeds) the reward keeps coming to you countless times bigger! I repeat: **it is harder to grow through what you are doing good deeds for yourself than to grow through good deeds done for someone else, even for your close ones**. Much more help comes back to those whose efforts go to helping someone else! Only then we can overcome ourselves and really understand our Savior, we are uniting with God- at that time we don't need to understand any more, to be "shaken" in order to wake up, we are on the Path which lifts us up and we receive whatever we need to go forward.

It is said that many entities from Heaven (angels, archangels, saints, etc) want to come back to a bodily life (to be born on Earth) because here, in the fight between right and wrong it is far more difficult to be good- this is the fastest way to grow, because it is very difficult to live between the two opposite poles: good and bad.

Up there, it is very easy to be good, because you're surrounded only by positive energies and good entities. But it is a great proof of spiritual force to be able to manifest good while being surrounded by evil! I've read what people who got close to the Other world wrote, they came back because they missed certain persons or because they still had unfinished missions on Earth. The hardest thing, when you leave this world is the reality of the fact that you haven't completed your mission and only then you understand how important it is for the soul to accomplish it and that actually, the way through life was wasted in sterile battles against those around you, with envy, evil, revenge. In reality we have no reason to fight each other- we each come with a different mission and we can help ourselves and receive greater powers for doing good deeds!

Although during our life we can be attracted to different persons with whom we would like to interact for some time; on long term we want as a partner a real man/woman, towards who to feel admiration, reliability, to experience a relationship based on profound values... We want a person who possesses inner and outer beauty, to delight us daily with noblesse, kindness, warmth and intelligence. This is why it is important for us to grow as high as we can and by becoming this kind of person we deserve such a partner, according to our own value.

I have always been amazed by the artistry of God's work: I don't think that God monitors each of us in every second of our life- we are His children and He loves us, He doesn't watch us waiting for a mistake to be done! I strongly believe that what we emit, the accumulated vibration through our action acts like a whole, generating a resultant whose value attracts, according to the resonance principle, some deeds/happenings/persons which we interact with, specifically to receive chances to correct our wrongs. It is only normal for those of us who have vanity problems, to have lower chances to receive a super appealing car or a very elegant house, because our vanity would crush other people around us. This type of people will experience numerous failures, till they will understand that their value is the same as the value of a poor person, that humbleness means power and wisdom and that there is no need for them to assault other souls to grow- we each come on Earth with our own personal mission, which becomes easy to complete if we help other people. Practically, by helping others, we are helping OURSELVES in the fastest way possible!

Going back to beauty, the most simple and fast way for constructing the grounds on which we can attract light entities (angels) who transform us esthetically, is the way through which we get closer to God and allow love to shine through us; the way in which we are putting fear behind us and regardless of what comes next, we have to trust the fact that we attract only what is needed for our future growth: if we do enough good deeds, we won't need "troubles" anymore to give us a wake-up call!

I have written some guidelines below to help us get the optimal inner and outer beauty of our body; these ideas are very much conditioned by the inner balance and beauty:

- Eliminate the resentfulness towards the way we look, we must learn to love our body- we are the only responsible for what we "have" today and it is up to us to become more harmonious, more balanced on an inner level and brighter; we must get rid of fear of not succeeding to be sufficiently beautiful, because everything we think and emit to the Universe becomes reality;

- Try to start your every day with a smile to the world, to yourself and to what you are about to become; look at yourself in the mirror and try to show an illuminating smile, from your heart- you will receive an aura which will make you charming; also try to smile during the day;

- Thank to God, to the angels who are taking care of your beauty, because as the days pass, you are closer to your optimal beauty, optimal silhouette, inner harmony and balance- this will bring you changes each day, which you will be surprised to see;

- Think positive, try to not envy anyone because you cannot know the problems of that soul and maybe it had suffered previously in order to deserve that "luck" for which you are envying it;

- Try to not hate and immediately forgive the ones who you think have harmed you- sometimes you must pity those persons, they are most of the time unhappy and unbalanced; try to help and forgive them with anticipation;

- Be gentle and kind, do good deeds that can help you accumulate the spiritual gold, that basis of luck from the future; today's deeds outline your future and I am sure you wish for a great future!

The most important thing is to start the journey on this path and the changes will be done gradually, by applying all the previous knowledge, which will help you to access the optimal beauty, but more important, you will emanate that light which will make you an admired person who radiates beauty, high spirits, success, glow and love.

There is a saying: "it is not beautiful, what's beautiful, beauty lies in what I like", that means that physical standards are less important, like: a certain height, specific measurements, etc; if a certain person is emanating beauty, she/he will magnetize everyone around him, will generate the desire of enjoying his/her company. So smile, do good deeds, forgive and treat those around you with conciliation and beauty will appear shortly after!

SAYINGS ABOUT BEAUTY:

"Beauty is the wisdom of women. Wisdom is the beauty of men" **Chinese proverb**

"No object is so beautiful that under certain conditions, it will not look ugly." **Oscar Wilde**

"The greatest treasures are invisible to the eye but found by the heart." **Anonymous**

"Beauty without virtue is like a flower without a scent." **Anonymous**

PRACTICAL APPLICATIONS

In order to do something more concrete than the previous advice, I suggest that in the evening, before going to bed, or in the morning right after you woke up, to say from your heart, with conviction, the following prayer:

"Jesus Christ, Son of God, help me live a life full of beauty, love and truth, help me fulfill my highest path, in order to live in harmony and love with those around me. I thank you, Holy Spirit, for helping me manifest more and more inner and outer beauty, do good deeds assigned to me through the Divine Plan, to fulfill as much as I can with Your Will! "

I recommend from my heart to start living the miracle of your transformation, by applying the advice written above **starting from NOW**. You will be so enchanted by the change, so at peace with yourself that every second dedicated to this new way of living will pay off! Life can be beautiful, we do not need punishments and challenges if we choose to live according to the Divine Laws, which also represent the Laws of this Universe!

CLAUDIA NITA DONCA

CHAPTER 6 - HARMONY

I have always been fascinated, both in movies and in real life, by the peace and self control of powerful people, either priests, actors or less known persons. I couldn't believe that there are people so at peace with themselves, who aren't afraid and don't get upset in a negative way, who are able to help others with their wise advice!

I have talked with such persons and I understood what was making them so powerful and fascinating: their inner and outer harmony of our soul. From what we have learned in our family and in our society, death appears as an ending, as "game over" for all our plans. After what I had learned from my spiritual searches from the last years, I understood that, in reality, death is a transition process between two roles, a process during which we have the time to rest our soul and to evaluate our wrongs and rights; so that we could start the next mission with the power to overcome our next tasks (these tasks are connected to whatever we haven't succeeded to accomplish in our past life). Death may appear when our future actions could not help us grow anymore or when we are very advanced, we have solved much more than we were supposed to in this lifetime.

Of course, there are also cases in which the personal mission can be supplemented, when a soul wants to remain in his present existence (although he had realized all he came here for), to help other dear souls, adding a plus of good deeds to those already existing. So regarding death as the "holiday before the next school year" (metaphorically speaking), we mustn't be afraid of the end and we must do as many good deeds as we can before this moment, so that we won't be sorry for going through life in vain! From what I've read about persons who experienced clinical death and after that, came back to life, it is very frustrating for the soul to see what it has lived and to realize that it has chosen for the wrong way, furthering away from what it had picked for himself before being birth. The barometer which tells us we are on the wrong path is the soul burdening, when we feel weight on our soul even if apparently we are supposed to be happy. When we are on the right path, we maintain the state of happiness, we enjoy small things and we feel as we are flying. There are divining methods to "measure", using as instruments the pendulum and the wire loop and draftsmen, how much we have accomplished of our present life's mission. I often do this type of measurements, but not to alert myself, but to guide my next steps.

Going back to fear (the one which generates our torment in those moments in which we want to act) - regardless if we are afraid or not, the result doesn't change only because we develop feelings of fear, on the contrary, it makes our personal mission harder. In fact, our inner harmony comes out of the total trust that whatever comes next is fair, according to the Divine Law. You must trust that what comes next will offer you the best part of your life, if our present actions are good, according to our personal mission. When our soul is burdened, we wake up with a general tiredness, those are moments in which we are furthering away from our personal mission and we must try to feel what we did wrong, to find the source of our guilt. The fastest way to get over this state is to help somebody, to do good deeds without expecting to be rewarded for it- immediately an unburdening will occur, we become lighter and more fulfilled. If we are feeling our soul light, we are cheerful and we feel the happiness, all these mean that our interior barometer indicates the fact that we are on the right path, we are doing what we must for fulfilling our personal mission.

Inner harmony helps us relieve stress, eliminate fear and accumulate a much better health state, based on trusting what tomorrow has to offer, trusting the fact that everything happens for a reason and that what happens to us is a consequence of what we emitted (the mirroring phenomena) because everything we emit comes to us, even if we sometimes believe that what we have done is not visible or that divine justice does not apply on Earth.

I like the next story about the faith in God: "there once was a man who lived alone between many others like him. Life seamed senseless and pointless even though he had lots of money, a beautiful house, many servants, etc, he would often watch his servants. He felt sorry for them, he pitied them and toldhimself, how hard must be their life as slaves... He enjoyed his freedom and money day and night... he partied with his friends, had many beautiful women, ate the most sophisticated foods. This was how he lived his life, while his servants were living a hard life... they lived in modest houses... they had to work daily... they had their laws, a specific way of living which seemed hard to stand to our man, all in all, on their faces you could always see a smile. But once, at a party, our man met with an old friend. And that friend looked him, in his eyes and asked him:

- Buddy, what's the purpose of your life? Our man had no good answer to offer… As the days passed by, this question kept repeating itself in his head… what was the meaning of his life… he had all he needed, and still there was something missing. He could not realize what he was missing, and so he went to look for a hermit and seek for his advice.

He climbed on roads and trails, walked through dark wildwoods through meadows full of light and on steep and frozen cliffs, where each step could lead him straight down to the bottom of the abyss. And finally, he got to the cave where the hermit was living… He got in, and sat down in front of the ascetic and asked him:

- What am I missing, father? The hermit looked into his eyes and said:
- You are missing a MASTER…"

When we have no objective, when everything happens without a purpose, life's joys have no value… when we don't know how to give, when we only know how to receive, we are furthering away from our path and from reality.

There are moments in life when we judge others around us, convinced that we hold all the details of a certain situation, but we can never know the drama lived by a person who we are envying for his/hers wealth, or for other reasons we are seeing as a simple observer. In reality, each soul is born and dies with its own lessons and fears, each person goes through life as he/she considers best and we have absolutely no reason to fight each other, because the lessons which come to us are the ones that we need in order to grow and fulfill our personal mission- so nobody is guilty for what happens to us, more than we are.

Regarding other people's acceptance in relation to what they do good or bad- because all these mean the life lessons needed by that soul- the story bellow impressed me:

"They say that one night, a boy who had just reached the age of 18 and took his driving license asked for the permission of his father to use the family's new car, to impress his girlfriend. The night was extraordinary, the car was running smoothly and he proved to be a skilled driver. On his way home, feeling that he could control the car, the boy wanted to see how fast can it go, but because of this he could not see a car stopping in front of him. And although he had stepped on the brakes, the impact could not be avoided. The result… the brand new car was crushed. The police were called and asked for his license and registration. "- What will my dad say?", the boy thought while opening the car's glove compartment. In that moment from the glove compartment fall a paper, which had written on it: "in case of an accident, son, remember that I love you, not that car. "

Our choices affect our future; each day we make different decisions, which eventually affect our future. If you choose to smoke, to be uncaring, if you choose to do a good deed, to help somebody, to tell the truth, to choose not to share it, because all these consequences will be visible... we will encounter what we have "sown". And in those moments we won't be able to blame someone else.

A state of acceptance regarding what is about to happen to us, according to our choices, is faith in God and the Divine Will; moreover, the optimism and kindness, humbleness and forgiveness are going to bring peace between us and everything surrounding us, giving us a state of health and power, which makes future possible lessons useless, only as long as we understand by ourselves. The state of fear or reluctance, the conviction that there is a plot against us generates a lot of frustration and creates a tomorrow which we do not want to expect and which we do not want to leave as inheritance for our children, for they will pick up our unfinished business.

Wisdom means acceptance and understanding, kindness for those around us and compassion for those who suffer and aren't able to understand, gentleness for the weak ones and help for those who make efforts to understand and transform their lives.

The good news is that everything we have talked about earlier isn't difficult to apply at all: on the contrary, the following life experiences become very beautiful, through a state of happiness, fulfillment and harmony with everything around, but most important through an inner harmony!

Friends will look for you because they'll feel very good around you, you'll be inspired, beautiful and you shall generate light and harmony around yourself...

Anything we are experiencing in the present is in accordance to our vibration, simpler said, with the level of good deeds done in the present. In the moment when we are doing many good deeds, our divine right grows, we are allowed to receive more and we'll resonate (in order to create harmony) with other place, other house, other job, etc. Practically our life will change, our structures will become more harmonious and more beautiful- we'll help our loved ones to change with us and then the whole Planet will vibrate differently- if everybody would accomplish our personal mission.

Harmony is related to the wisdom of understanding that regardless of how much we worry, things have a dynamic sense based on the cause-effect principle: whatever we generate comes back to us as a consequence and as long as we fight results without changing our emissions, we cannot reach harmony because we'll always consider that we are victims of a certain state, that we had bad-luck, that things did not go in our favor... Actually everything that is happening to us is a consequence of what we are doing and as soon as we get this, we can balance our inner part and we shall use our energy to change ourselves starting Now.

I was once asked by a friend of mine how I can be so calm, smiling daily and appear so at peace with everyone. I answered that I understood that the state of good attracts good and from a little ball in the beginning, you can build a great source of optimism and cheerfulness. Usually we condition ourselves in a negative way by telling our sorrows over and over again, insisting on what brings us pain- but any problem which exists today, can be transformed rapidly by tomorrow in an achievement, if what we permanently emit is trust and optimism.

A very suggestive joke comes to my mind: the pessimist said: "it can't get worst than it already is!", while the optimist said: "yes it can"! Everything is possible: your today's greatest problem can be solved in a miraculous way if we have faith; or vice-versa, when we are convinced that we are more important than everybody else, a problem may occur and "bring us back on Earth". The solution is to not torment ourselves so much for the days which are about to come and to emit good thoughts, unconditional love, kindness and conciliation from inside, and you'll see how the "magical wand" changes everything it touches.

When there is inner harmony, troubles pass us by, because they have nothing more to teach us! When a lesson is no longer necessary, because we've understood it before its arrival, we are surpassing that obstacle and we're more understanding, we are becoming wiser. And life's so beautiful when we are not wasting our energy on negative thoughts, on envy, on selfishness and fear… we are starting to see people differently and they are attracted by a harmonic soul; they will permanently search for your smile and wisdom.

"They say that a long time ago, lived a very good squire. One day, he called for a peasant and told him:

- Look, man, because I know that your family is challenged, I want to help you. I am giving you work to do and I am paying you very well. Do you want to work for me?

- Of course, squire-answered the man happy- what do I have to do? - You have to build me a house, on the fringe of the forest. The peasant walked happy and on that same day he started working. The squire gave him money for everything he needed to buy. But the peasant thought: "What would it be like if I would cheat him as long as he doesn't notice?" And instead of doing everything as he should have, he started buying cheap things for the house and spent the rest of it on personal needs. When he finished building the house, it was looking very nice on the outside, but the peasant knew it wouldn't last for long. When he showed the house to the squire, the latter one said:

- Because I know that you and your family are living in a small shack, I am giving you this house as a gift. That's why I left you to build it and told you now, in the end, so that you can experience a greater joy.

Only then the man realized his mistake. He wanted to cheat another man and he ended up cheating himself. If he had been honest, he and his family would have benefitted from this situation. Now, his sorrows couldn't change the actual situation. So the man swore an oath to himself, never to cheat on anybody for as long as he lived."

Moral: God will treat us just like we treat our peers.

I propose you to start by being calmer, analyzing everything with maximum attention before bursting with fury or before judging someone for a bad thing that happened to you. Then, in the evening, when you get home, apply **"the screeningmethod"** which I've read about in Dan Seracu's books: when you are calm, lie down on your back, with your eyes closed, and visualize the scene which irritated/aggrieved you during the day; regardless if you have hurt someone or if someone has hurt you, remember, like looking at a screen, the negative scene which took place during the day; then imagine that scene disappearing (fading away) in to the left part of the screen and then visualize the perfect scene, as it should have happened in the ideal situation from your point of view. Do you know what will happen? All the energies implied by this deed/happening will rearrange themselves according to the ideal scene, bringing peace and tranquility for you but also bringing a healthy basis for the relationship with that person.

If you want to be sure that everything will come into its rightful place, say a prayer for forgiveness with the person with which you had a conflict. You'll see how, starting with the next day, your relationship with that person will get better and better: the state of harmony sets in and all the negative energies disappear.

SAYINGS ABOUT HARMONY AND POSITIVE THINKING:

"Keep your thoughts positive, because your thoughts become your words.

Keep your words positive, because your words become your behavior.

Keep your behavior positive, because your behavior becomes your habits.

Keep your habits positive, because your habits become your values.

Keep your values positive, because your values become your destiny. "
Mahatma Ghandi

PRACTICAL APPLICATIONS

In the morning or in the evening, when you are feeling tranquiller, say from your heart, with attention and love the following prayers:

"Heavenly Father, until this day I haven't been wise nor instructed, but I can see my mistakes and I am ready to make them right, Please, offer me Your forgiveness. From now on I want to be in harmony with You. Send me Your light so that I wouldn't brake your Will. Allow me to complete You. I will listen to you, understand you and fulfill Your will. Amen. "

After this you'll address the Angels and the Archangels: "**Many times you've came to bring me messages from the Creator, to warn me or to enlighten me, but because I was overwhelmed by passions, I didn't hear your voice. Please, continue bringing me light, because I want to listen to you. I know you are the greatest servants of God, I respect and love you.** "

These prayers will help you understand what is happening to you, why you are experiencing inner peace, why you are accepting whatever you receive and they'll help you understand that these all are happening for your highest good. Be sure that everything transforms in your favor, like a touch of the magic wand which helps you be better from NOW on!

CLAUDIA NITA DONCA

CHAPTER 7 - PHYSICAL HEALTH

Our state of health is closely related to our capacity to forgive, to getting rid of repeated sins, conflicts and unforgiveness. Through forgiveness these energies, which suffocate our body, are cleansed. These energies generate an unbalance which appears in the beginning in our energetic structure and then in the physical one generating illness.

It is important to understand that firstly, the energetic body is unbalanced and after a certain period of time named **recess**, the physical structure is unbalanced, therefore the first signs of the health problem appear. If we learn to eliminate those energetic residues after each day that passes, full of thoughts, deeds and words, both good and bad, then we are learning to maintain our health at a normal level and we are becoming our own doctors, without medicine and suffering.

It is a fact that some diseases appear, especially the complicated ones, as a consequence of some karmic payments and therefore we cannot fully explain how we "inherited" them. That is why it is so important to purify the structures through forgiveness, through inner reconciliation with whatever happened before, through good deeds and a healthy basis from now on; but any disease can be bettered though a radical change of the patient in cause. Through the important steps which need to be followed there are:

- Complete and unconditional forgiveness of those who we feel we had/have upsets; as soon as we understand that all the unforgiving from the past only dig into our health and happiness, as soon we set ourselves free from them.

- The acceptance of any situation less positive for us, by seeking to understand which are the causes, what we have done wrong and how to not throw the guilt upon those surrounding us; everything that comes to us is what we "deserve", remember the "mirror phenomena" I was telling you about at the beginning of this book.

- The cleansing of the energetic residues which appear as a consequence of the thought, word or deed (for example judging others, gossip, envy and evil, fights and accumulated tensions) at the end of each day; in the practical applications part I will explain to you how to do this.

- The understanding of the fact that as we are doing good deeds for other persons, we shall clean our karmic payments and earn the right to be happier, healthier, to become more prosperous, to be more successful.

- The change of our nurturing way, offering our organism more vitamins, fibers, offering it the needed rest; there are persons who rest sufficiently in 5-6 hours and others who need 8 hours of sleep - there is no general rule, but I can tell you that exaggerations aren't benefic for the organism; nature is a great place for it to heal, receiving from the inanimate nature a precious help which we usually choose to ignore.

In the cases where illnesses appeared out of karmic consequences, the solution is not to blame ourselves for what has happened in the past or for what cannot be explained: **all we have to do is to resolve our current problems**; regardless what we might have been at a certain point, the solution must come NOW. That is why I recommend you to forgive in advance what might have happened, all the people who have ever harmed you, because now these persons are surely not happy; if you seek for revenge, you are entering a new karmic row which will bring you suffering in the future. So in this circle, the person who forgives in advance is the winner, regardless of what he was or what he had become; the solution is to look forward!

If we consider everyone, from the beginning (just like in the story with the dog who goes into the mirror room) as being good persons who need help and who occasionally do bad things because they are tormented and unhappy...What if we would give those people a hand instead of hitting them? What do you think would happen to us? Most certainly somewhere, in the cleanest chamber of our soul a salt is produced, everything inside us is transformed and the change becomes visible on an exterior level, making those around us ask themselves how come we have become calmer, more interesting, brighter and more beautiful!

Good deeds never go unrewarded, by doing this we are manifesting our love, understanding, compassion, our status of sons of God and the consequences shall appear shortly after.

"A poorly dressed woman, walked into a grocery shop, she had a defeated look. She got closer to the shop's owner, in a very humble manor, and asked him if he could offer her some groceries for which she would pay another time. She explained that her husband was very ill, he could not work and that they had 7 children to feed at home. The grocer looked at her with superiority and asked her to leave the shop immediately. Thinking of the needs of her family, the woman said: - Please sir I'll get you the money as soon as I'll can. The grocer said he couldn't sale on credit, because she had no credits in his shop.

Standing next to the counter there was another costumer, who heard the talk between the two. The client took several steps forward and said to the grocer that he would pay for the costs of whatever that woman had to buy.

The grocer asked reluctantly: - Do you have a shopping list? —Yes sir, answered the woman.

-Ok, said the grocer, than put it on the scale and I shall give you merchandise as heavy as your list is.

After hesitating for a moment, with her sight facing the ground, the woman put her hand in her bag and got a little piece of paper where she had written something in a hurry. Then she put the paper on the scale, with her sight still facing the ground. The two men present were amazed by the fact that the scale was leaning toward the part where the piece of paper was. The grocer watched the scale, turned back towards the client and mumbled: I can't believe it!

The client smiled, and the grocer started to put groceries on the scale. The scale was still not balanced, even if the grocer had filled it with food. The man stood shocked and watched the scene. Eventually, he pulled the piece of paper from the scale and looked at it with great amazement. It was not a shopping list, it was a prayer: <beloved God, You know my needs, therefore I am handing them to You.>

The grocer gave the girl the merchandise and stood there petrified. She thanked him and went out the door. The other client gave the grocer a 50 dollars bill and said: "- it was worth all the money! Only God knows the weight of a prayer."

Our physical health is degrading as we burden ourselves with hard feelings, hatred, blame, judgment. When we forgive and accept that every man manifests a clean part, as light of God manifested through him; that no one is exclusively bad without suffering and without being tormented, it will be easier for us to UNDERSTAND and FORGIVE, just like God forgives us and loves each of us, like a patient parent! If we understood how much we are protecting ourselves and our health by accepting and forgiving, we wouldn't burden ourselves with these negative energies.

What's encouraging and important is the fact that, even if we did something unjust regarding other persons around us, or misunderstood, judged and hated those who harmed us, starting from NOW we can change every past event: through forgiveness (asking and offering forgiveness on an inner level) we can change both our relationship with that person as well as our well-being, including our health state.

Even if we realize our mistake at the last minute, we can straighten things; we cannot eliminate negative energies which we emitted around us, but we can neutralize the negative effects by substituting them with love, understanding, forgiveness and acceptance energies; all these will set us free, we'll feel lighter, happier!

What helps us in improving any health problem is an analysis of a list with the persons who we have sorrows and to look upon these relationships with light, we need to understand that we are the main responsible for what is happening to us. Through reconciliation with those around us and with ourselves on an inner level, our health state will get better. Forgiveness and reconciliation mustn't necessarily be done through direct communication with a specific person - it is enough to occur on an inner, sincere level. The next step is to "cure" what we bring from the past, this the difficult part, because we don't even poses the necessary information which can clarify what we have done wrong. The solution is to begin the karma healing through unconditional forgiveness of whatever happened wrong to us before and to forgive all those who have wronged us and made us suffer in the past. The results regarding the karma healing are not obtained on the spot, but from the moment you start working at this process, the whole Universe will cooperate!

SAYINGS ABOUT HEALTH:

"All people want to be healthy, but they often do everything against it." **Latin proverb**

"Health is not valued till sickness comes." **Thomas Fuller**

"To avoid sickness eat less; to prolong life worry less." **Chu Hui Weng**

"There are lots of people in this world who spend so much time watching their health, that they haven't time to enjoy it." **Josh Billings**

"The greatest wealth is health." **Virgil**

PRACTICAL APPLICATIONS:

I will mention again the prayer for forgiveness from the first chapter:

Prayer for forgiveness:

"Jesus Christ, I ask for forgiveness with all my soul, and all my being to ...... for all the harm that I have caused him/her in the past, I forgive ...... for all the harm that he/she has caused me and I ask forgiveness to the Holy Trinity for all negative messages sent out in the Universe. Amen!"

Quick cleansing of the structures at the end of the day

This form of cleansing the energetic residues accumulated during one day is so simple to apply, that you could use it at your work place, on your floor, for all the spaces where you and your loved ones are walking in.

Practically, you are imagining a shimmering white light beam, which comes from the Divine Source (God) and wraps you up, washing away every negativity; in this exercise the intensity with which you regard this "cleansing" of the structures with God's light, is very important, by visualizing yourself clean and shiny; this is a visualization exercise, which attracts whatever we imagine if our intentions are good.

You can apply this exercise to any place/space where you are or where you are entering: you have the right to stand into God's light as many times as you can. Moreover, it is very pleasant for light entities (guardian angels) if you often do this exercise and you'll feel their help when you need it.

If you get used to applying these exercises daily, you'll get to optimize your day, to feel more energy running through your body, to be happier, you'll obtain your optimal silhouette, you'll radiate light and it won't take you more than an hour a day!

I can't wait till you share your results with me (I will give you an email address at the end of this book), I would be twice as happy: once because I can help someone to become happier in this passage through life and twice because we can communicate, in the beginning through emails, in order to help you not stop here, but to progress together in the future! I sincerely believe that everything happens for a reason:

By helping yourself to start a more beautiful life, we are all balancing for a cleaner Planet for us and our children!

PRACTICAL APPLICATIONS

PREPARATIVE PRAYERS:

Heavenly Father

Heavenly father, consoler
The spirit of truth, present everywhere
You who accomplishes everything,
Treasurer of all good and life giver
Come lie within us
Cleanse all our evilness
And forgive our souls.
Amen!

Mercifulness door

Open for us the door to mercifulness
Blessed Virgin Mary, mother of God
For us, the ones who believe in you not to vanish
But to redeem of our needs through you,
For you are the redemption of the Christians.
Amen!

CHAPTER 1 - FORGIVENESS

Prayer for forgiveness:

"Jesus Christ, I ask for forgiveness with all my soul, and all my being to ...... for all the harm that I have caused him/her in the past, I forgive ...... for all the harm that he/she has caused me and I ask forgiveness to the Holy Trinity for all negative messages sent out in the Universe. Amen!"

CHAPTER 2 - HAPPINESS

"Jesus Christ, son of God, I thank you for the day that is about to begin for me, for the circumstances and optimal interactions, for fulfilling my mission and my personal growth, I thank you for the help you are sending me on every level, in order to have the power to fulfill the my path and find my inner peace, I thank you for the love I'm receiving and spreading, for accepting to manifest through me! Amen!"

The perfect prayer of grand masters

The perfect prayer, which is never refused by God because it follows another Universe law, is the one through which we give thanks to God for whatever we are wishing for! Our belief in Him is repaid and we are receiving exactly what we are wishing for, if our wishes do not imply harming others! For example if I wish to receive the gift of kindness, I thank God for my kindness, for being calmer, more at peace with myself and this gift shall come soon... We only have to be grateful from the depths of our soul and be convinced that we shall receive whatever we are asking for. I have applied this method and I can assure you it works! And you can use it in any domain, it has the same efficiency!

CHAPTER 3 - LOVE

To parenthesize, I have found out through different attempts in the past years, that everything we are imagining determines the future and, why not, the present. I mean, if we visualize in our mind (with as many details as possible) that a certain action takes place, this is most likely to happen, because it comes through that anticipated faith according to which God offers us whatever we want, if we do not harm others with this action. For example you want a certain car and for rushing the process, you will imagine the moment in which you are actually buying it, with the excitement you feel when driving it for the first time, with the details about the color, type...

Accordingly with your trust in these beliefs, the ways to transforming them into reality will appear. In the same way, as an example, if you made a mistake and you've hurt someone badly, firstly you can imagine the real side of the story, which happened and then you can replace it with the story you wish to implement, the ideal one. The negative energies generated by the action you wish to avoid, will be cured.

Prayer for love/the loved person

"God I wish for a man/a woman, to get along with, to be my confident; I wish so much for a person, to love and to love me back! Help me God, to meet someone suitable for me, someone with serious intentions, a life partner. I want to love, to make someone happy! Watch over me, Lord! Give me the power and the longevity of your love and protect me forever! Amen!"

I've promised a prayer which I recommend to all of those who have decided to make an abortion. I suggest saying it daily, until you feel liberated from thinking of those little souls. I suggest to you, as a mother to seek help also coming from your priest, because the light will get to those little souls in this way.

Prayer for the aborted souls

"I am blessing with the love of God the souls of my aborted children, I ask for their forgiveness from the bottom of my soul because I have rejected them and I ask forgiveness from the Holy Trinity for all the evil that I emitted in the Universe. I am asking our Savior Jesus Christ and Virgin Mary to help these souls rise into the light, accordingly to the Divine Will. Amen! "

CHAPTER 4 - ABUNDANCE/WEALTH

Prayer for money:

"Jesus Christ, Son of God, I thank you for what I have and for your help in obtaining the money gain which I deserve thanks to the divine right! Untie, God, with your light and power, my money gain, of any aggressions did against my free will and give me God wealth, happiness and gain, to fulfill in an optimal way my life mission! I thank You God for the abundance and the gain in money and help me God to do with it whatever suits my path! Amen. "

It is possible for the light angels who deal with our money gain to be tied down through our past wrong actions (we were greedy, and gained great sums of money without deserving it). By saying the previous prayer faithfully, each night, with gratitude for what we have and for what we are convinced we are about to receive, the energies opposed to our divine right will be eliminated.

CHAPTER 5 - BEAUTY

In order to do something more concrete than the previous advice, I suggest that in the evening, before going to bed, or in the morning right after you woke up, to say from your heart, with conviction, the following prayer:

"Jesus Christ, son of God, help me live a life full of beauty, love and truth, help me fulfill my highest path, in order to live in harmony and love with those around me. I thank you, Holy Spirit, for helping me manifest more and more inner and outer beauty, do good deeds assigned to me through the Divine Plan, to fulfill as much as I can with Your Will! "

I recommend from my heart to start living the miracle of your transformation, by applying the advice written above **starting from NOW**. You will be so enchanted by the change, so at peace with yourself, that every second dedicated to this new way of living will pay off!

Life can be beautiful and we do not need punishments and challenges, if we choose to live according to the Divine Laws, which also represent the Laws of this Universe!

CHAPTER 6 - HARMONY

In the morning or in the evening, when you are feeling tranquiller, say from your heart, with attention and love the following prayers:

"Heavenly Father, until this day I haven't been wise nor instructed, but I can see my mistakes and I am ready to make them right, Please, offer me Your forgiveness. From now on I want to be in harmony with you. Send me Your light so that I wouldn't brake your Will. Allow me to complete You. I will listen to you, understand you and fulfill Your will. Amen. "

After this you'll address the Angels and the Archangels: **"Many times you've came to bring me messages from the Creator, to warn me or to enlighten me, but because I was overwhelmed by passions, I didn't hear your voice. Please, continue bringing me light, because I want to listen to you. I know you are the greatest servants of God, I respect and love you. "**

These prayers will help you understand what is happening to you, why you are experiencing inner peace, why you are accepting whatever you receive and they'll help you understand that these all are happening for your highest good. Be sure that everything transforms in your favor, like a touch of the magic wand which helps you be better from NOW on!

CHAPTER 7 - PHYSICAL HEALTH

Quick cleansing of the structures at the end of the day

This form of cleansing the energetic residues accumulated during one day is so simple to apply, that you could use it at your work place, on your floor, for all the spaces where you and your loved ones are walking in.

"**Jesus Christ, I ask for forgiveness with all my soul, and all my being to ...... for all the harm that I have caused him/her in the past, I forgive ...... for all the harm that he/she has caused me and I ask forgiveness to the Holy Trinity for all negative messages sent out in the Universe. Amen!**" Visualize yourself clean and shiny; this is a visualization exercise, which attracts whatever we imagine if our intentions are good.

CLAUDIA NITA DONCA

CONCLUSION

How are you feeling?

Every one of you who walked with me through the pages of this book is very dear to me, because there is something uniting us: the desire to create a better life for us and for this Planet. If each of us became better, cleaner, more prosperous, more beautiful and more harmonious I think that our life would prolong and it would become more serene and full of joy... I also think that God would smile, being proud of His children.

Most certainly everything happens for a reason and if something you have learned from this book will help you live better, awaken inside into your highest reachable level, it means that you deserve to receive these gifts! Life can be beautiful, we must only keep our eyes "open" so that we could "see" it.

Children transmit us many wise and clean ideas, we could learn a lot from them, if we wouldn't be preoccupied to "educate" them with so many prejudices which limited ourselves as children. I remember something nice: when my little girl was three years old, she overheard me one night worrying, because I had to make a pretty big payment, a tax, which I couldn't fit in my existent budget. She looked deeply to me and said, looking into my eyes: "Be calm, the Mother of Jesus will help you!" I knew she was right, I had received a sign through her, the belief that I shall be helped.

On an inner level, it helps to acknowledge that any sorrow, dissatisfaction, unrest, has a purpose, because we attract towards us only what we need in order to grow: if we attract problems, it means that we receive a sign and that we must seek inside ourselves the mistake. If we are on the normal path, we'll feel it through our achievements; our soul is the barometer: if we feel lighthearted, we are on the right path, we are growing, but if we feel burdened, clearly we are stepping away from our optimal path, from the personal mission assumed by us for this life.

Pay attention, there are persons who try to burden us, who feed on our kindness, common sense and with our inner gentleness, trying to take advantage and to make us feel guilty when we cannot offer our help. When you don't know how to react, say a prayer and then take a look inside you, in your soul and see what you are feeling in the firsts seconds after you asked yourself a question. Those thoughts are the clean ones, from your pure self; regardless of the following question marks, you must have the courage to follow your soul: for the soul is the spark from God which we've received at birth as a legacy, the purest part in every one of us.

There are divining methods for "measuring" many of the important aspects of our growth:

- Our personal vibration: if we are lower than the planet's vibration we must make greater efforts to grow, because in this way we are helping the general growth;

- How much of our personal mission have we realized till this moment and how much of our personal mission have we realized in this lifetime;

- How much are we respecting God's Will through our actions;

- Which is our divine right to money: how much are we allowed to earn;

- How much have we already paid from our karmic debt;

I often do this kind of measurements, not to alert myself, but to guide my future steps and to understand my pluses and minuses. Besides this, when problems appear, these minuses can explain what I have to do to correct the existent situation. Also, when you have to make important decisions, it is very helpful to find constructive guidance, with the light of God through which to see everything clearly and to go forward armed with courage.

I've decided for the following period of time to start doing therapy, to help people not only with advice and clarifications about what is better to do next, but to correct the diseased energetic fields and structures and to raise with God's help all of those who come to me and who are suffering. But one step at a time, I will dedicate more of my time to therapy, if by this I can do more good around me. Also I would like to get involved in realizing light initiations for the persons who want to grow, in order to be more protected and helped by the spiritual guides who can barely wait to be involved in our growth and the Planet's growth.

I have been feeling for some time an urge to write down all my teachings and practices accumulated in the past 7 years of development of my spirituality; I felt that I could do more, that I possess inner power and faith, I was seeing how my life was improving on every plan, although the past few years haven't been so easy on me. One night, after thinking how I could transmit all this knowledge to other people, I had a clear dream, where someone very kind and gentle was telling me to write down everything I am feeling, as if I was teaching someone close to me everything I know, in order to help that dear person to lead a better life...

At the beginning I didn't think I was capable, but when I wrote the first word of this book, ideas came flowing, as if someone was arranging them in my mind and on the page. I felt a huge help and inner peace, as if each page I wrote brought peace into my soul.

What I want now is not to stop here, but to walk forward together. I trust that we can live better, be healthier, be more beautiful and be more understanding with those around us, if we all learn to be wiser, diligent with our priceless possession, our soul.

Thank you for being patient while going through these pages, for trusting and helping me to reach your most valuable little chamber, the place where the "magic wand" is, which transforms our lives... It is important to know that whatever you want to achieve is doable, never back down and trust your soul: it is enough to truly want something and the whole Universe will cooperate!

"Learn from everything

Learn from everything to have a steady way,
Learn from flames that everything's just ashes
Learn from the shadow how to shut up and listen,
Learn from the cliff to stone-still believe,
Learn from the sun how you must set,
Learn from the stone how much to say,
Learn from the wind which blows through the paths
How you, through life should quietly pass,
Learn from all that everything's your sister,
How you should go through life,
How you should die."

I am sending you all my love in order to go forward together, with courage on Our path!

May God help us!

Claudia

CLAUDIA NITA DONCA

ABOUT THE AUTHOR

Claudia Donca has graduated the Academy of Economic Studies – Marketing in Romania and holds a Professional Diploma in Marketing UK (Chartered Marketer).

Ten years ago she has started the spiritual growing, accessing also parapsychology knowledge. Being Master on many spiritual systems like: Reiki, Karuna, Gendai, Shamballa, Melchisedec, Divining- level 7 and using communication skills developed over time, Claudia has proposed to apply the acquired knowledge and provide those who need it, those who want to grow spiritual.

She has worked 17 years in multinational companies (senior level in marketing) and now is practicing holistic therapies to those who need it and she proposed to reveal everything discovered that can lead to a better life, to all her readers.

Contact
e-Mail: contact@viata-mai-buna.ro
Web site: http://viata-mai-buna.ro

11796094R00039

Printed in Great Britain
by Amazon.co.uk, Ltd.,
Marston Gate.